BEYOND LOSS

A Path from Pain to Peace

Geraldine M. Ryan

iUniverse, Inc.
New York   Bloomington

BEYOND LOSS

A Path from Pain to Peace

iUniverse books may be ordered through booksellers or by contacting:

iUniverse
1663 Liberty Drive
Bloomington, IN 47403
www.iuniverse.com
1-800-Authors (1-800-288-4677)

Because of the dynamic nature of the Internet, any Web addresses or links contained in this book may have changed since publication and may no longer be valid. The views expressed in this work are solely those of the author and do not necessarily reflect the views of the publisher, and the publisher hereby disclaims any responsibility for them.

ISBN: 978-0-595-44835-7 (pbk)
ISBN: 978-0-595-89155-9 (ebk)

Printed in the United States of America

iUniverse rev. date: 11/26/08

Dedication

To my son, Joseph, my heartbeat.

Forward

In the years that I have known Gerry, I have been witness to her battles with extreme sadness and depression and her victory over cancer. While there were many days and nights when Gerry struggled to surface for breaths of air, they came, one at a time, irregular, but frequent enough to keep her lungs full and her head above water.

During the more recent years I have been a witness to a mother's love soaring, an ex-wife's reconciliation of what was and what was supposed to be, a grandmother, so proud, and a dear friend to me and others. She would share the treasures that she had, her stories, her "string of pearls," her pearls of wisdom.

When I first read "Beyond Loss," I was touched by the honest simplicity of Gerry's poetry and language. The themes that I found highlighting the travels in her journey were that love transcends fear and that life, like the roads of her precious New England, takes it's own toll.

Gerry shares with her readers, she confides in them, she trusts them; she guides them with her stories of broken dreams, the unknown and what is verses what was promised. Gerry also endorses love, as the major healing force in her life and of the universe, and it was and is her love that has touched and strengthened and at times healed the people dear to her. While love is pivotal in her world, she also talks earnestly about love lost, barren love and lovelessness.

While it is apparent by Gerry's writings that her road traveled has had many speed bumps, pot holes, tolls and tickets, she also points out signs along the way to help out her fellow travelers. "Beyond Loss" is to me a road map of Gerry's thoughts and feelings, wishes and worries, questions, quandaries and observations. She gives her readers proper signage, pointing out dangers and hazards, as well as wrong turns and dead ends, with the hope, I think, not just to write poems as a collection of memoirs, but of a string of pearls of wisdom for them to perhaps gain insight, connect with and identify.

Gerry leaves no rock unturned in exploring her own garden. She has weathered the hard times and grown throughout. She has planted seed amongst weeds and rocks yielding a hearty oak who has shot up and survived many storms, and that oak has spread seed too. Her son, Joseph, who is a fisherman and Captain of his own craft on Cape Cod, is that mighty oak that she nourished and so dearly loves and wants to protect; and he has proven himself time after time as a good son and devoted father. Motherhood for Gerry is a precious and love-driven duty to buffer her son against the fears and trials life has to offer and to share the joys and accomplishments also, as read in her poem, "Lullaby."

Gerry shares boldly in her poem "Feelings," that while there might be physical attraction between two people, with a yearning for physical affection, that this can be a solitary process - not breaking loneliness as one might think but contributing to a more intense loneliness. In the poem "Karen," Gerry bravely refers to the "... endless searching at the banquet of loneliness." In the poem "Victim," she declares that love can mean pain, and where are her protectors; her promised knights in shining armor? Do they live only in the fairy tale dreams of young naive girls?

In the poems of Geraldine Ryan's "Beyond Loss," I find her being refreshingly candid, giving me insight into her life and times, a gift from a person who has taken on many roles: mother, wife, ex-wife, daughter, sister, friend and counselor. Gerry shares with her reader that, while her life experience contains failed promises and dashed expectations, it has also been a full life, rich with love, and pleasant surprises. It is full and rich because she chooses to make it so, despite her obstacles. I am honored to call Gerry Ryan my dear friend. We have survived many turbulent times, while also experiencing times of joy. I am delighted that she has decided to publish these moments of insight and growth.

Charles Weinstein, LMHC
Adjunct Instructor
Cambridge College, Cambridge, MA
University of Massachusetts, Boston, MA
March 23, 2008

Acknowledgments

In my past there were two superb women, "Aunt Barbara" and "Gramma Roche," who taught me how to love... unconditionally. Because of them and their examples, I have been able to give and receive love on my journey toward peace. Knowing them sustained me many times on "the path," and continues to bring me joy, courage and wonderful memories.

Loren Schechter, another very special human being, my friend and mentor of many decades, has earned my ongoing love and gratitude. He helped me find the path when I could not and encourages me to stay on it in my life's journey. His friendship and sharing our experiences warm the cockles of my heart! Thank you for being there. Thank you for your wise perspective. Your kindness is legendary.

Of my many dear friends I must specifically mention Marcie Dahlen, my college roommate and role model, who has been responsible for much of my mental and emotional health over the years! Thanks for so much loving nurturing, Mar. On that note, I acknowledge Chuck Weinstein, who has been there for me seemingly forever as well, and who graciously agreed to write the Forward to this book. Our friendship has spanned many years of joyful as well as tearful times. Thank you, Chuck, for your steadfast humor and generosity. Lest I forget, thank you high school friends; and Joanne, Karen, Lauren, Jaime, Jay and Kevin for the tears and laughter. I love you all.

While preparing this book for publication, I have been especially fortunate to have Chrissie DiPietro at my side as friend and agent. She created the outstanding cover for the book and offered some very important editorial suggestions during long hours of work together. Chrissie's hard work and firm foot at the base of my spine were most helpful when I got frustrated. Her efforts, along with the publishing consultants at i-universe, brought my dream to completion. How can I ever thank her enough?

It goes without saying that I am fundamentally grateful to my loving family for their confidence and support in my efforts. My son, Joseph Weinberg, and grandchildren, Nicholas and Grace, are constant joys and challenges. They make for interesting times during my mostly peaceful life on Cape Cod. My brother, Thomas Ryan - the other half of the sad story - is always there for me. I know I can count on Tom as confidant and cheerleader. Abby, Erin, his son-in law, Dan, Tom's daughters and his grandchildren, Jack and Kia May, add tremendously to the happiness of family life. Aunt Patty and numerous cousins to see at our family reunions round out a happy picture of my family.

Life has often dealt me a difficult hand, but the family, friends and mentors I have and have had, more than make up for the struggle. I extend appreciation and gratitude to all.

PART I

Loss

Finality

Once upon a dark
       night searching
fell the craft, stilled
       the films
stole the Bud
blight to the bush
beyond the waters
dreams be fulfilled.

Fantasy

Space
I caught your face
you were there
I touched your hair
so fair.

Your smile
I had you a while
you're in my heart
we'll never be apart
a part of me.

Tangible

"Gerry"
there's my name
on the nose of your plane
fame?

A link to the past
the nose was smashed
and I lost my only you
my fame, my game,
my name?

No not me
cheri.

Target

How long before you
knew it was over
was there time to sort it out
fear, anger, helplessness
did you and your shipmates shout?

Was there time to know
was it worth it
in spite of a very short course
time to know you'd left
life behind
or were you one with your Source?

And was the impact blunt enough
to end all fear and pain
and could the loss which
stripped us bare
no longer be our bane
to haunt again, yet again?

Ocean

Water
caressing my skin
consoling my pain
refreshing my spirit
it's better again.

And, a coffin
a place to be with you
a union of souls
eternity triumphs
or maybe black holes.

St. Avold

A military grave
outstanding in the stark
      white logic of endless rows
      horizontal, diagonal
penetrating the quiet, peaceful
      rolling French countryside
the awesome, gruesome
      majesty of a government's tribute
homage to a warrior slain.

I'd rather have you back.

PART II

Reflections

Seelisch gestoert

You came to meet me as I returned from Metz
        but why
were you tuned in to the rumblings of that hour
        there in your silent protective way
        had you missed me
did you sense the burgeoning, vast steppes
        within my heart?

I could never tell you how overwhelmingly you loomed
        in the electric eye of my soul
        did not understand myself
        but felt.

Had you just been able to reach out and
        scoop me up in your tender arms
        hold me fast
        save me from the folly of girlish fears.

But no one's charisma stretches that far
nor would protect the unprotected...
you knew I would not happen back
        despite the letters
your anger shreds my gut even now
        wounded, merciless, hard
and I...
        struck dumb
to feel only the cavernous, bleak death of
        the abandoned
the unspoken dread of losing you forever.

You?

But not happening back
does not cancel the happening.

With every vision of Alpine splendor
every toppling of an Argentine regime
every remembering snapshot of my mind
the wonder of our may-have-been
          lives together
floods my senses.

The reality of what is
sometimes crushes my joy, awhile
I only need you to find your place
I still care enough to shrink from
          "seelisch gestoert"
to want better
peace.

John M.

"A bag of toys," he endearingly called me
I knew it was an accolade
but missed his cue.

Now, many years too late
I yearn to tell him
what he means to me.

Why is it that time gets in the way
why can't I go back
and make it right?

Why don't you answer my letters?

Karen

"Would you leave your husband for him?"
she asked, no words wasted
how to explain…

breaths of cherished moments
strung together like
pearls on a silken thread
quicken the heart's beat
stoke the imagination
warm the flesh
tingling with joy, anticipation, and aching

then, the business of the days
reality shaping the hours
purposeful, productive
familiarity affords firm footing
security, a fabric for surviving

the craving of the spirit
endless searching only to find
starvation at this
banquet of loneliness?

Victims

To all of us for whom love means pain
whose caring and worth turns to horror and shame
whose trusting feelings become deep blame
and what of a child's sense of honor?

Bumbling along with outstretched arms
continually reaching for love's lasting charms
blindly ignoring the hurt and the pain
and what of a child's innocence?

With good intentions we start out
to laugh and giggle and dance and shout
with dizzying speed we turn about
and what of a child's confusion?

It makes me crazy to feel the pain
of a loveless life, no sharing, no flame
to continue as victims "rejects" they claim
and what of a child's desperation?

What of a child with a mind and emotions
that won't work together in harmony and devotion
striving to make it, deny painful notions
and what of a child's forgiveness?

Can we count on ourselves, I must ask
when scattered, and feelings become shattered glass
is there no way to mend the constant blasts
and what of a child who feels helpless?

Where's the protection, mutual respect
the right of a child to give and expect
the things that surely our whole lives affect
and what of a child's understanding?

Unconditional love, will we ever feel that
'cause feelings, my loves, are just where it's at
a mind is useless with just pure facts
and what of a child feeling hopeless?

Can we count on ourselves, I must ask this
to commit to love, does it really exist
is there such a thing that can help us persist
and what of a child's dreams?

Work with purpose; learn who you are
don't ever forget that twinkling star
that shines on me and you from so far
and what of a child's wonder?

Love is a strength we must nurture inside
reach down deep, tap it, take it in stride
it's all around us and deep in our hides
and what of a child's consolation?

It's out there, I know it; erases the pain
it's wholeness and wellness and strength to gain
the freedom to think, then plan one's game
and what of a child's control?

Love moves me deeply, brings out such tears
helps to console and control morning's fears
no barriers here, acceptance from peers
and what of a child's reaching out?

Forgive ourselves our past mistakes
love demands the effort this takes
free ourselves of the intense breaks
and what of a child's heart?

I won't forget moody and blue
hope I can pass on to you
the power and strength of my vision, it's true
and what of a child growing up?

The pain, I hope, will slowly subside
for all victims loving within and outside
learn, heal, encouraged, time patiently bide
for what of a child's glory?

Shame

Dawn comes again
shrouded in grey
covering my sin
with its grip

                    trip

                            trip

seizing my being
tomorrow is now
function again
but how...

grab yourself, woman
don't flip with the trip
just 'cause you want him
doesn't mean shit
it's just special moments
bite the bit

pull in the reins
tighten the slack
he'll need you for now
and that's the goddam flack
but the draw between us
what does it mean…

his lips on mine
his tongue a soft blade
don't take it slow
make me glow

please…

you reached me pal
I wasn't lookin'
a bomb went off slowly
and now I'm cookin'
and alone.

Jeff

I truly wish I could buy you a yacht
but make you happy
I think it would not
hell, the best of Life's in the
battles you've fought
and won

you struggle to make the pieces a whole
who are you, why are you
gain mastery and control
another reason
merge the poles

forces from outside; wars from within
the struggle goes on
you think it won't end
you'll just need a boost
reliable friends

I love your combo of
impulse and thought
vulnerable, tough
considerate, then not
powerful yet sweet
mysterious, open
wonder in your eyes
distrustful, distressed
baby, you can fly
try

soar above the conflicts and worries
touch the sky
this you can't buy
it's yours for the taking
don't ask why
freedom

life is a smorgasbord, taste it all
it's the pace that can wear you down
create false walls
it's just…living is so damn complex…

I could cite chapter and verse
yeas, nays, ifs, and buts
back 'em up with wherefores, therefores,
      sweaty pores

and give it a rational explanation
but...

for grave and other reasons
you are in my life
I'm definitely not complaining!

Seeking

You're really classic
classy too
afraid to let it show?

Let it glow
grow
maturity becomes you.

You'd be surprised
old man with a thousand faces
enhanced with a thousand graces
magnetic, charming traces
pull it all together
treat it lightly as a feather
use it wisely.

I don't want to lead you on
nor do I want you gone
forever
it's just that the truth can set you free
not that there are guarantees
but I've always been comfortable with honesty.

Reality brings pain and joy
life just isn't a barrel of toys
but we do have choices
can change our minds
correct mistakes
make new ones.

I catch a pool of sadness
behind those wet, blue eyes
it's not unbearable
not so bad
just for the moment
time to regroup
to recoup.

In the meantime, play and enjoy
the game of the girl, the game of the boy
'til there's a powerful love in your life
and a song in your heart
never to be apart.

Sweet

A day came and with it
thoughts of you
brimming, bittersweet
thoughts of us
eyes, brimming.

You left and left me
thoughts of you
confusion, hurt
thoughts of you
patience, comfort.

Some months passed, and with them
thoughts of you
kaleidoscopic, colorful
thoughts of us
friends smiling.

Some years passed, and with them
thoughts of you
a chameleon yet warm
thoughts of us
special people.

Moments

I'll fly with you
a trip to the moon
for these short moments
will be over too soon

you'll fall asleep
my head on your chest or
your head on my breast
peacefully

we'll wake to the sun
relaxed, a new day
smile at each other
tease laugh and play.

All is well.

PART III

Peace

Earthmother

You told me clearly by the light of the day
to go away
I'm not blind
 I have a mind
occasionally filled with common sense
won't you at least come say, Good-bye?

Play me a tune on your guitar or my flute
talk to me, write something, give me a hoot
aw-w-w shoot
isn't there time for that?

We connected for moments; it really was fine
we both like to glow with these moments in time
desire surfaced, but didn't take off
but your lips sure are soft.

The ball's in your court
I don't like to force
an issue.

God's in you and also in me
we know what feels right and go with it
when free; we'll see.

Older, yes. More experienced in what?

Technique, magic buttons
passion...I think not.

Just another earthmother, curious and yet
searching for answers from those I can't get
tired of searching; I want a home
something of substance I can't find alone
I really do think such a thing does exist
you'll know and I'll know when not to resist.

Your life is a challenge; hold on to that thought
you've got the stuff, to have or have not
you'll have your day, you've taught me a lot.

And you are fascinating
but not for the taking.

Nurturing

How is it that she came to be forty-eight
before finally confronting her demons
were the first forty-eight wasted?

No, my dear.

She packed it on and took it off
as if a fuzzy wuzzy teddy bear
hibernating in the winters of her soul
waiting to be held
securely
by someone.

And when she was not hibernating
she foraged in the hills and dales
and moved on.

She swam like a fish and rocked in
Mother Ocean, the womb of the Earth
she played games with her loved ones in this
       playground Paradise
       free and flowing.

She wore a cocoon and produced a butterfly
       colorful
       a real beauty
but that wasn't all.

She nourished her Being in the
          flowerbeds of the earth
forever seeking Beauty, Goodness and Truth
taking care of what was there
          as she could
she learned about nurturing
lest the flowers die
and it was not their time.

With her Jesus sandals
          and wool-warm cloak
she went the highways and byways
searching
always with a white knight at her side
and an earthmother to cling to.

There are many paths to God.

Reflecting upon her roots
she came full cycle
with love guiding her
a new understanding
another white knight
in the service of the Lord
aiding and abetting - abbe.

For all the sons, brothers and fathers of the world
he came like a thief in the night
and stole my heart away
he'll treat me gently and with kindness.

Love.

John K.

You should know my Lancelot
I'm lost in his studied stare
the gentle pleasure of his face once again
perhaps he is aware
the promise he holds fast within
to bestow come some timely dare?

Of a sudden, the now of a moment
he reached out and strummed my chords
and the song goes on to sustain me
as I wait for Sir Lancelot, Milord.

Future

Takes a lifetime, they tell me
to protect how you feel
to have scars like iron
which help you to heal.

A time will come when you'll not
feel so pulled apart
your mind will grasp Life
fueled with your loving heart
      harmony
      no fear.

You'll be a superlative piece of work
my special friend
an awesome mosaic
wise and whole to the end
but never boring!

The Patriarch

I'm not complaining that life's not fair
'cause you came along full of warmth and care
since twelve you have guided me, patiently there
sensitive, watching, protective, so rare.

You've given me memories, Europe to see
fun at the Erwins, fun places to be
material things, warm cups of tea
I love you Pop, and I know you love me.

You took care of Joseph; you just stepped right in
your love of my son was a blessing, we're kin
you worried about his life and limb
as he teetered and tottered on the head of a pin.

You passed on your knowledge and wisdom, too
my precious piano, another gift from you
your heart's on your sleeve, tried and true
keep sending those prayers as you kneel in your pew.

We've shared a great deal with years more to come
there's lots to be shared still before we are done
my Pop's an Ace, equal to none
hardworking, loyal, generous and fun
a very special one.

James

"Is he coming or at least calling?"

"I don't know."

"Doesn't that drive you crazy?"

"Not particularly."

"Describe him to me."

Blue, sparkling eyes
penetrating, sure
cloudy when stressed
but never a bore.

Long arms...tall
I have to reach up to him
hugs so sure
it's nice to see you, Jim.

Wonderful hands
a gentle touch
a true Irish brother
I care for him much.

To me he's protection
when I go astray
a true friend and loving
when I come his way.

He comes when he's troubled
he comes when he's spent
he comes when his tenants
don't pay the rent.

He opens up slowly
cautious with ties
he thinks about you
and then says, "Goodbye."
he tries.

I love how he mingles
and tangles with all
who come into his life
who bring something and call.

He's a father first
and never forget
his business brings purpose
deep meaning, and yet...

He travels his pathways
and thinks about things
considerate, then not
happiness he brings.

I ask him everything
I need to know
he's patient with me
in his now-and-then glow.

He shoots from the hip
I know he'll be honest
he's very secure
and no con artist.

Loneliness plagues him
isn't that where it's at
for all of us, searching
for something down pat?

Serious, judgmental
he should have more fun
but I don't know surely
I just squeeze his buns.

His joy is his boat
I guess at its meaning
I stumble, he's there
to catch while I'm leaning.

His face is alive
when he is afloat
carefully managing
his castle, his boat.

It's just such an honor
to take the wheel
he's a wonderful teacher
and wonderfully real.

I've seen his changes
for seven years now
he's older, he's wiser
he's sharing now...Wow!

He travels his pathways
carefully he pays
the price of friendship
the knowing of ways.

The work of relating
a coming together
emotional bonding
some ties to sever.

I'll always need him
such a sense of protection
I need him to calm me
and give his affection.

"That's Jim."

"O-h-h-h."

Loving

"Outrageous!"

"Really, John, and you?"

Armed with a breakfast tray
splendid with crystal and
daffodils.

A newspaper under your arm
you'd flood my room with
warm, bright sunshine
read me the days highlights
then quietly disappear
leaving me to my meditations.

With such charm you pampered me
made me feel lovely
encouraged my endeavors
enlivened my spirit
fostered my hopes.

Did I help
make it any easier to
struggle with your You?

I struggle, too
and prize your memory
and miss your slow
      low
           chuckle.

Delight

You built me a chapel
a skylight, as well
my penthouse, a guestroom
a prison, a hell…
a monk in her cell?

I lie on my back, upside down, looking out
sun, moon and stars
what's it all about?

The sun warms my bones, as I search the sky
peacefully lying there, clouds passing by
an occasional airplane brings memories, not tears
that was all yesterday, today no more fears.

The moon sets the stage, an emotional glow
remember, while baying, go with the flow
stars so magical sprinkle the sky
sparkling, winking - I won't pass them by.

Planets so wondrous, Ancients come to mind
the wisdom of Ages…the dawn of mankind
sages, psychics, Spiritual Guides
am I really so blind?

So many images, as I fall asleep
peaceful, relaxed; tomorrow will keep
loving you.

Yellow Butterfly

He saw it once before, while sitting at my side
a beautiful, yellow butterfly
hovering over a bed of orange-warm
tiger lilies.

I told him later that, years ago,
sitting before my guru, I had asked
"What will become of me
when I break out of this cocoon?"

And he had replied, with that warm twinkle
in his eyes…
"Perhaps a butterfly!"

And we laughed together, though
with much skepticism on my part
at the joy this image brought.

For some time, I collected butterflies.

Today, he told me he saw it again
that same, yellow butterfly
delicately nestled
among the bright, sunny flowers.

So special did I feel
another tentative connection
and I smile at our shared image
a gift of God and Mother Nature.

Daydream

If I were a clean, white seashell
    lying on the purest sand
you would love me as I am
    simple beauty, grand
you would touch me, gently hold me
    wonder in your hand
    grand.

If I were a bottomless pool
    waiting in a quiet glen
you would love my cleansing touch
    seek refreshment, not too much
    peace.

If I were a crystal globe
    dangling in the rays
different facets everywhere
    sparkling and ablaze
you might be amazed
    magnificent.

If I were a catchy tune
    whistling through your day
you might find my cheery notes
    help along the way
    happy.

And if I were a wounded robin
    fallen from the nest
you might sweetly raise me up
    help me do my best
    love.

Blue Geese

A swoosh of sound parting the sky
   to burst in a breathless spray
Cinderella's ball gown?

  Na-h-h-h

But it's blue and white
and fairy tale bright
and full of a magical, princess-type night?

  Na-h-h-h

Well then, a cosmic shot
into the dark
spewing mysterious sparks?

  Na-h-h-h

Then, consider Hope with its
cool, pure flow
eternally promising?

  Na-h-h-h, oh-h-h-h...

The Sea

There's an entity out there, like no other
in some ways She is me or like my Mother
in other ways, She reminds me of you
unpredictable, warm, powerful then blue.

I visited Her this morning very early
cold, damp and grey, her mood was surly
only the sound of Her lapping the sand
soothed with the rhythm of Her familiar hand.

Gentle, white-capped, She touches the beach
rolling back slowly, you know She'll retreat
you can't rely on Her to be calm
of a sudden She'll change and maybe do harm.

Why do I love Her? The range of her ways
expressing what's in me, reflecting the rays
consoling, mysterious, depths you can't plumb
yet beckoning me to Her to come.

Crashing on cliffs with strength, perhaps rage
tossing boats here and there, just a small gauge
I love her majesty, She's a survivor, you see
Her beauty is there for you and for me.

I go to Her when I'm scattered inside
I go to Her when there's pain in my hide
She's always there, and She's always a trip
somehow She helps me maintain a tight grip.

She doesn't lay guilt, nor does She find fault
She is what She is, a mysterious vault
in spite of Her changes, She calms me and tames
I'll always seek Peace from that magnificent, old Dame!

Birthing

What do we have, here in this cell
circles of orange and blue
trial by fire and water
breaths of Life, Truth, and you.

Walls so bare, mysterious, gay
shelves filled with complex things to say
a jail keeper, watchful, all-seeing eyes
piercing my walls, death to all lies
we'll strip my attic of excess baggage
strengthen my wings, I'll fly.

"Life is struggle" the keeper puts out.

The struggle is not without but within
not with others, but with oneself
to sustain belief that it matters
one's life, one's strife.

Behind it all lies this presence
eyes penetrating, blue
clear, honest, waiting
baby it's up to you.

Yeah, I know; it's always been that way
but if you only knew
how ever-lovin' grateful I am
for you and those eyes of blue.

'Cause every once and so often
'specially in times 'a hard pain
those blue and orange circles
keep it all going, the flame.

And the brown, veiny arms of my chair
hold me tight
keep me there
scouring the depths
grief, sadness, tears
those old blue eyes soften
lighten the burden of years.

No, Sir, you can't be replaced
you're etched in my hopes and my fears
a jailbird's been protected
someone was there to hear.

In place of yesterdays wasted
tomorrow, with bright hopes and dreams
freedom to sing and to dance about
that jailbird stays right on the beam.

True, never there was such a jailer
though bars between us do lie
can one really measure the gift of breath
light, faith, tools to survive.

Can one really thank a guru for that
never-found-joy, I'm alive!
for conspiratorial humor
for sensitive path-finding dives
for a gentle lifting up again.

Hey, you guys, I've survived!

See, in the beginning a part of me died
that's been like an albatross deep in my hide
now, sure it's still sore
from my head to the core
but we've turned it to fuel for the ride!

Lullaby

Mummy, I'm so scared.

And well you should be little one
for all that lies outside that door
but listen, hear, and heed my words
for the love between us sure
for what I want the most for us
is feeling love secure.

Come and sit upon my lap
I'll wrap us tightly in my red, wool shawl
and touch the golden threads it has
how warm and bright, don't fall
we'll read of kings and queens and knights
and other tales as well
I love to hear your tiny voice
it rings just like a bell
we'll sing of twinkling stars above
of sheep and crooked things
and feel so close together here
safe feelings true love brings.

I can't protect you from the world
or things that make you lonely
but please remember how special you are
I look and see you only
I'll love you always my gypsy child
even when I send you off
beyond that door to find your life
to struggle, puzzle, and laugh
to make your home a happy place
to find work that's rewarding
to have friends near and dear to you
and strength to keep it going.

There is no perfect trust or love
for we are human beings
so now, I'll say, 'I love you much'
forgive me my human dealings
forgive me for the pain I've caused
never would I hurt you
but there are times I feel confused
mistakes do hurt me too
put aside those awful fears
of ghosts and ghouls and other's jeers
I'll be there for you as best I can
with shouts of praise and tears.

And so, my little, gypsy child
go on your way well knowing
that I do love you in a special way
I pray to God you're growing
growing tall and free and strong
unhappy as you may be
for there are rainbows in our lives
that beckon to you and me
you'll find your pot of gold and such
and use your power for good
to share or not, as you see fit
in a world of brotherhood.

Your eyes are heavy, it's time for sleep
your little fists unclenched
I'll wrap you up in my red-gold shawl
now dream of love unspent
search out those dreams and make them real
find what you really need
keep yourself together and well
and never stop searching, Godspeed
remember the knights of the Holy Grail
remember those who weep and wail
be true to yourself and you'll never fail.

I love you.

Future

Takes a lifetime, they tell me
to protect how you feel
to have scars like iron
which help you to heal.

A time will come when you'll not
feel so pulled apart
your mind will grasp Life
fueled with your loving heart
harmony
no fear.

You'll be a superlative piece of work
my special friend
an awesome mosaic
wise and whole to the end.

Purpose

In the Autumn of my life
in the peace of my home
I learn the best is yet to come
healing myself and others with care
the beat of the drummer I hear in my ear
my day is far from done.

All is One.

And I have things to do.

Haiku

shadows filter through
forest glade alive with sun
mystery abounds

powerful and free
winds whip wildly through the leaves
Mother Nature reigns

multicolored rows
garden beauties evoke charm
pink, white, purple blooms

alligator there
among massive roots in tree
creatures manifest

Printed in the United States
131888LV00001B/11/P

9 780595 448357